MILKWEED FOR MONARCHS

Seraphim George

ISBN: 979-8-9998878-0-1

꽃

To my children, Sofia, Isabella, and Ezekiel,

the greatest poems I am helping to write.

May they grow to be monarchs among the milkweed.

INTRODUCTION

I have come to believe that true life cannot be found apart from suffering. I don't mean the shallow difficulties we sometimes call "hard" because they inconvenienced us. I mean the kind of suffering that strips you bare, takes away what you thought you needed to live, and forces you to see the truth of who you are and *why* you are.

Most people, if they are honest, will say they'd rather avoid such things. We spend whole years arranging our days to sidestep discomfort, pain, and loss. We build our lives around insulation; better jobs, safer neighborhoods, careful schedules, familiar patterns, anything that keeps us from being broken open. And yet, for all our planning, the breaking comes anyway. Sometimes it comes like a sudden storm. Other times it works slowly, wearing you down grain by grain until you finally notice you are changed.

If we run from it, we lose something essential. A person who spends their whole life dodging pain might call themselves fortunate, but deep down they are still untouched, untempered. They have not been tested in the fire, and so they have not been remade. They may live long, but they will not truly live.

The natural world speaks this truth everywhere, if we are willing to see it. The seed does not become a tree by lying safe and dry in the palm of your hand. It must be buried in darkness, cracked open, and forced upward through cold soil into unfiltered light. Rivers do not carve valleys by drifting gently through them. They cut their way with floods, wearing down stone over centuries until beauty emerges. A caterpillar does not grow wings by wishful thinking; it allows itself to be undone inside the chrysalis, remade in ways it could not imagine.

I believe this is no accident. It is not simply the way nature "works" on its own, as if it were a mindless machine. The Creator made it this way, as a mirror of His own story. God Himself entered His creation, not to avoid pain, but to embrace it, to redeem it. The same hands that shaped the galaxies allowed themselves to be pierced. The same Word that spoke the world into being was silenced under the weight of the cross. There, in the greatest act of love the world has ever seen, suffering became the doorway to life.

If God wanted to keep His distance from pain, He would have left us to face the consequences of our ruin. But instead, He chose to step into the cold soil with us, to take the flood upon Himself, to enter the cocoon of death so that when He rose again, He could bring us with Him up into open skies. This is the pattern He set for all of life: death, then resurrection; winter, then spring; sorrow, then joy.

This is not theory for me; I have lived it. There were seasons when I thought my story reached its end, that everything that made my life worth living had been taken from me, that I was left with nothing but the hollow shell of what I was. I could not see how God was working in those years. I could not imagine anything good growing from the scorched ground I stood upon.

But He was there, as silent as seeds in soil, as patient as a tide that wears down the rock. He was remaking me in ways I did not understand. The pain did not disappear overnight; some of it has never left. But in its place, something else began to grow: a steadiness, a clearer vision, a joy that could not be taken from me because it was not built on the things I lost.

These poems grew out of that journey. They are not all about suffering, but they all grow from it. Some are rooted in specific moments of loss or disorientation. Others reflect the small glimmers of light that came afterward; the way the sun strikes a certain field in winter, or the way the ocean moves under moonlight, or the way a milkweed pod splits and sends its seeds into the wind. They are bound together by the same thread: the conviction that life, *real life*, is born from the places we would have never chosen to go.

That is the heart of this book. That is the heart of life with God. We are all, in one way or another, monarchs among the milkweed: taking in what we would never choose, trusting that the Creator who made us will bring us through, and rising one day into the wide, bright air we were created for.

- Seraphim George

TABLE OF CONTENTS

WHERE DRAGONFLIES COMMUNE

I sit under the pine tree,
hidden, observing from a bench
the sanctuary past my house,
down my road, a mile round the bend.

The scene is saturated green,
sun-light dapples dance between trees
swaying over clover, straw, and grass,
where dragonflies commune with bees.

I am lost in the smell of earth,
wood, moss, and fragrant flowered herbs,
lost in winged patterns of swallows,
the sea of reeds the wind disturbs

across an open field. Its waves
of light race across its surface.
Behind it stands a forest wall,
epic in stature. In that place

the mystic, columned hall is formed
with woven roof, and below,
a thousand flowers grow in groups

like white blankets of summer snow.
Here, I forget a mile off
the scent of gasoline,
and metallic, noisy, man-made things
dash solitude to smithereens.

DEMETER'S CALL

It's January still,
but you would not know it,
except for trees which stand
now nude and sunbathing
in an extraordinary
interruption.

Persephone escaped today,
heard Demeter's call
and through the earth rose up,
reached out onto the surface.
She touched it,
just before her husband
pulled her back to Hades.

Sitting in her fingerprint,
the smell of spring unnatural
but welcome.

Like the bogs before me,
stripped and dull, yet having thrown
a remnant to their edge along
the sallow turf, this is
a day incarnadine, not dun,
a post-it note for spring.

EARTH CHILD

Little verdant child,
peering out
from underneath
a peaky, woolen blanket.

The clouds had tucked her in.

She wakes because she hears
the Father's call.
Soon she'll be arrayed
in floriated fashion

and coiffured
with iridescent jewels,
prepared to greet
the saffron sky of spring.

FISH MONGER

The walls are dark-stained wood, the bar the same,
asking my imagination to recall
the days of fishermen and whale men,
and now those men of old have lost their claim

to oceanographers and sun-burned tourists.
Heavy smells linger here, of fresh-caught fish,
burgers, French fries in the fry-o-later,
which spatter grease and toss a savory mist

into the atmosphere. Conversation,
heckled with the interrupting clang
of silverware and plates, orchestrates a hum.
In front of me, a screen quilts a pattern

on the windowed scenery, letting in
the salty, seaweed air. Just outside,
water blankets up against the weathered docks,
bathes the land and salted population.

This place is a clever disinfectant,
cleansing zombish minds, like mine, of stress.
My sandwich comes. The waitress gives a smile,
mumbles something nice and turns, tip-expectant.

BIOGRAPHY OF AN ANT

A movement on inverted granite sky
with hair-like legs that escalate behind,
a foot to go, for him a thousand miles.

A one-ton crumb lies upon his shoulders,
fallen from an old man's decrepit hands
giving bread to doves to find his meaning.

Some instinctual beast-call, some duty
to the Mother causes it to stumble.
And to what end? Think of it.
His obstacles are harder to defeat

with that bread crumb. The sun, through glass upheld
by youthful brats, has baked his kind before.
Now it beats on him with birds who hunt,

who watch his way, wait patiently to strike.
The food he carries doesn't help his case.
For pity's sake, it makes them drool the more.
And where is this wayward traveler's home?
The hole is near. He senses it, feels it,
the instinct of another draws him there.

But though he doesn't know exactly where:
like Poles Point or Chatham Light or on the Knob
off Woods Hole Way, his path is marked off well.

I hope he lives. From here I cannot tell.

HARBORED STORM

Falmouth Harbor lays before me, tortured,
confused, abused by an arresting unseen wrath,
uncharacteristically whipped up.
Thrown upon the dock, cold and violent

waters weave pandemonic wave with wave
and form an agitated, anxious spread
of foam and rippled bedlam, thrown over
the abysmal secrets of the sea.

An air-brushed expansion of foam, unrolled
from me to the Elizabethan Islands,
writhes in the likeness of the sea below.
The smooth, slate and undulating mass

of unshed storm, despairing its burden,
vehemently seeks to let it go,
rolls onward vexed and frustrated,
to the place where it can be released again.

I sit between the dismal sea and sky,
tossed by the same impassioned winds that blew
the clouds and surf, bewailing me to tears,
and like the setting, splitting me in two.

THE FLOATING WORLD

I am alone, like a willow tree
cut off at the root. I want to float
where the water flows to take me.

Clouds sail on a sea of constant blue
while day after day the sun rises,
then falls to the onslaught of the moon.

Like them I just go on, drifting,
drifting like the colored maple leaves
floating down the frosted wood-streams

of Bourne Farm and yellow fields of straw
adrift upon the autumn breeze,
before the coming of a bitter snow.

SIGHT SOUNDS IN NEW HAMPSHIRE

While in New Hampshire God makes men,
it's in her woods He lets them play,
with cool-mist carpet cover,
and rain washed gorges strewn over the earth
in an aquatic madness paradise,
long-winded droplets all reflecting proof
of singing ground, dancing water
spinning by and wisping faces
licked, crying inadvertently,
avalanche of train noise swollen
on a granite bubbling track,
and through it all, the lost river falls.

STRANGER IN THIS LAND

The truth: it is who I am,
a stranger in an old, forsaken land.
On our ship, my captain steers and I,
through wind tossed seas just stand

and wonder how this blemished,
lifeless land was once a golden shore.
A stark disquiet issues from my heart,
for I've been here before

and remember once not long ago
I also lived on this unhallowed ground,
but left upon this vessel found,
whose captain had unbound

my heart, immersing in despair,
and caused my blinded eyes to plainly see,
I'm a stranger in this land: who I am,
who I was meant to be.

POINTERS

Jump left. Turn right. Now run
along the russet shore
where wood meets gilded fields.

Their masters run behind,
blowing into wind the whistle calls.

They follow
spotting birds
escaping
into aromatic sunset smells
of earth tone tamarack.
They run, ears flopping,
palpable excitement
galloping like horses.
They stop. They point.
Good dog.
They wag their tales
and run through endless
sunburst possibilities.

They are confined by rules,
calls, commands,

but I envy them.

They are free,

bound in chains

among their masters.

I long to run and catch birds,

to be free.

OF WAKEBY POND

He's dead, underneath the agued coffin-lid,
The static, blackened vault of Wakeby Pond.
I heard through friends his dog deceived him once,
Seducing him onto the ice at dawn.

Winter played her part, reassuring him
The blanket, spun with winter's thread of frost,
Was safe. He trusted that maleficence,
Who hides in peaceful white, a blackened rot.

Now the spring has rules which haven't changed.
The beauty here: the birds, the trees, the brisk air
Disguise the morbid truth of what occurred,
His bloated, banished body lying still, out there.

The waves of saw-grass chill when thinking how
He feeds them now, invigorates their growth.
Dancing on their captive, mocking that they've won,
They drown him once again in muck-draped root.

But wait - Perhaps his sleep is not so bad
On pebbled bed, with rush's rooted spread.
And when he wakes he'll see the mingled sun,
Distorted sky, and shadowed feet of swans.

'SCONSET

Melancholic cottages in droves
scramble for the sea in layer
tumbling over layer,
splash on stilts upon the breakers.
They flatter the sea, a mimicry
of shingle over weathered shingle,
gray as the Nantucket dawn,
riddled with cracks and dents and grooves:
products of wind and time
like a battered wave's surface.

Time passes. Observations fly.

No more distinct, the masses
fall united with the deep,
each cottage a wave,
each street a current,
each rotary a whirlpool,
around which white-capped houses swirl,
each block a gale,
the village a tempest.

I walk between the crests

with friends, with villagers,

with other traveling guests,

who float upon the sea:

the sea at 'Sconset.

ON SIX FOOT WINGS

I am surrounded by celestial beauty,
overwhelmed by mountainous expanse,
the vulture's dance
on six foot wings upon the snowy wind.

I have met Elijah's ravens
souring up to cavernous nests
of sticks and tamarack,
as if they come to feed me
on the mountain's barren peak,
black angels of God,
messengers from a holy realm
to keep their eye on one
alone.

RAIN

Hear the rain as it falls to soothe the soul
By sound and music, a saturating choir
Of wet and shifting light. Old river's refuse,

Having once fallen, rises, ascends upward,
Glorified and waiting for its coming
Twice again, and after, parachuting down

To rest in tingling ears and bladed grass,
Filling gutters round the roof, and rushing proof
That rivers run again. Can you remember

entering its sun-soaked after glow,
Marveling the subtle pearls and wet jeweled plants,
A ragged dance of prisms, lost in new sun's light?

Rainbows live there, in Noahic after-light,
Like covenant's peace, still and meditative,
Come as promise after forty days and nights.

And that same rain rung in the patriarch's ear,
Heard by millions a hundred thousand times, then
Heard by you. Perhaps tonight it comes again.

CROSS OF GOLD

A rambling fold: crinkled, gold-dry.
Rumpled out to touch
the blue-nipped cool horizon,
a bed sheet ruffled, settled by servant hands
in the making.

Urbanite pursuits, rent, crucified
on a cross of gold
to hang fire in sunlit winds,
a motile tomb of irrepressible
self-expression.

THE FALL

It runnels through
a cool New England wood,
a serpent slow and silent,
until it gathers speed
to lash out at my feet
a hissing spattered spate.
I am crippled by
its venom, struck to the heart,
impelled to watch it wind
into the tawny
tamarack and nettle.
Its dapple-scale skin
tessellates the lambent gaze
of an autumn sun.

THE ALBATROSS

The water slaps, slaps, slaps
like a woman's powerless defense
against the plowing
forward motion of the prow.
Above, riding high
upon a wood-wave's crest,
the grizzled salt-man
leans like an albatross
in strong Nor'easter winds,
master over the reflected world,
dominionist
over Nature's acquiescence,

breaker of whales
and souls.

ACADIAN WAVES

Waves shepherd me
into your kingdom,
empire of mist, light
and holy places,
saturating souls
and bringing dew
to arid spaces,
until I'm overcome,
sprouting tears like shoots
from weather-beaten rock.

THE SEA BY TENNYSON

What sea, that dances on the furrowed moor,
Could quell my sorrows, quench my fears as this,
When, stretching out from me, only to kiss
The mouth of some as yet unchartered shore?

My mind does wander from this precipice,
Beneath this ocean, playground to the free,
Where mysteries and beasts of darkness be,
Rising from the fearful, blackened-blue abyss.

And now I sit to watch the setting sun,
Where sea and sky and light become enmeshed,
My spirit, knowing it will be refreshed,
The world's woes a little more undone.

SURF

Thunder has been done to death.

Rather, it is the response
of arrogance to war:
an applause that drowns
the cannons
of war,
both sounds mingling
in violent approbation.

Sizzling
pan bacon
seething, searing
in its grease.
Leaves whoosh
in a thousand
forest shades,
countless ruined
poems tossed
away.

The waves
leave water-veins

within a golem's

tawny skin,

trickling

down,

inhaled

by the

swell,

until the thunder comes again.

And at the crash, the water billows up,

a white cumulonimbus

racing over golden plains of rock and wheat.

Behind the cloud,

an aquatic sky

of liquid jade:

a peace,

translucent

in the sun.

The milk from water,

a first miracle

more tame,

more subtle

at the place

of fumbling froth

and ochre rocks,

spread thin,

like cobwebs

swept across

the mirror's glass.

DESCRIPTION OF THE SEA FROM A BOAT

The very color blue is shaken,
fractured into countless shades,
tumbles, crashes, and disperses
one within the other, symbols
of divine magnificence, a sacred
revelry of light and wet and sky,
every body panting to delight.

In God's making, unseen hands
knead the water's swell, a dough
that, when mixed with sun and surface-play
will turn to awe and bliss and praise.

And there's no land. There hasn't been
for days, yet how is it that I feel
grounded, like the seagulls scattered
on the wind, kites that hover
in their hundreds, ride the seaweed smell
of brine and sickly rotting fish
and salted air, yet feel secure there,
as if they stood on solid ground.

WINDOWS

Outside the windows fly
of another world, another life,
window to window passing
like strangers, like light wintry airs,
inconsequential, unrestrained.

And trees, buildings, people,
the harbor tweaked with moon
and pale lamps, fraternal twins
that dance upon the waves and time,
pass like film along the glass,
along the cool rigid touch
of a translucent gaze
into a transient companion
of a world, until it disappears.

All of it: all this dies,
is buried at my back
under the soil of my periphery
never to be raised.

And if I turn

it is altogether something different:

changed and running away.

I think of death,

of passing lives and trees

and windows.

A MIRRORED IMAGE

Like a school boy's whistle
at a passing girl, the bird sings.
Crayon-yellow breasted feathers,
bright orange beak, folded black wings
mold the bird. It repeats its cry.
Within, it calls to me.

The brush bounces, moving suddenly
above the tiny tree-topped glass.
A sacrificial sight appears:
a moth flaps desperate in the grass.
The bird falls quickly on its prey.
There is a breeze today

ruffling my clothes as I watch,
disheveling the finch's feathers too,
as it enjoys its catch alone.
Back to the water's edge it dips
its head, spoons the water lightly
lifting up to wash it down,

repeating silence once again,
making sure the bitter taste of bug

and fleshy crumb consumed.

Then it stills, looks at me, flies away.

I'll leave as well, a woebegone

disconsolate to wander.

LIKE HUMANKIND

In a tense and violent storm
the great tree fell. I saw it,
lying in his throes.

I thought then of the cycles
during which he stood, patient there
in his appointed place.

A thousand times or more, the tree
beheld the earth and burst to bloom,
amid the happy songs

of mating birds. A thousand summers
beautified his flesh with a crystal
crown of jewels,

beaming in a shifting storm's sun.
And every night for all those years
he stood alone

upon that hill, rogue and silent
in the lonely light of a white
and mystic moon.

WAKING FROM A DREAM

When I leave the island, without fail,
I feel as if I'm waking from a dream,
stuck upon a vessel somewhere sailing
in the moon and morning.

I see the dream, a distant sunset haze
exhausting form and breadth and color,
captured in between an Eden lost
and Purgatory gained,

bound to lost ideals of peace, nostalgia,
longing and fulfillment, faith in God,
who conjures light from utter darkness
smoldering in the void.

When I leave the island, without fail,
I feel as if I'm waking from a dream.

WALKING UNDER STARS ON NANTUCKET

Walking under stars on Nantucket
I am a lone lighthouse weaving beams
with night air, beckoning to ships and angels.
In the utter darkness I'm unafraid
of creatures roaring from the sea,
of angry dunes cast by shadows
with my flashlight, furrowing their brows
as light moves across the sand, meets shadow,
and they disappear.

Unmoved by my blind periphery,
I'm guided rather by the smell of brine,
the sound of depth.
Here, I see with my heart and come to rest
on mist-wet sand that clumps between my toes,
cool and unchained.

But even now, through the darkness,
clarity begins to seep
into the understanding of a night.
The stars begin to cast their ancient light
and the surf explodes upon my vision
in froth and violence and ghostly apparitions
that coalesce and then recede.

NANTUCKET

I

Nantucket: island of my heart, within
its rhythmic soundings lost to the pulsing
of the sea's perimeter, throwing up
its sand upon the waves, as a white flag
in the calm anticipation of peace.

Placed within a body of dark terrors
and beasts of unfathomable power,
where storms dance over a lachrymose floor
in intemperate worship, uncaring,
unanswerable to anyone but God.

II

People school like fish
upon its shores
in search of food
strewn across the cobblestone,
of shelter, of friendship.
Every year they swim
on surface sands,

inelegant

yet lithe, a sign of safe

discomfort, a turbid light.

Like clouds they come

to carry off the sun,

dissipating

on the ferry home.

III

The Lady Grey

vanishes from sight,

with a glimmer,

a wink and a nod,

in the exhale

of a dying sun.

THE GREY LADY

Do I sail away from her,
or does she sail away from me?

Subsumed in fog, she floats
upon a still, sleet ocean,
vanishing within a swath
of mist and magic,
the ghost of a dream,
not terrible or lost
but melancholy.

She's like a lover's body
lost to endless fathoms,
beautiful and still,
becoming less distinct
and sinking down,
down into the depths
beneath the surface gray.
A final strip of sand
that glows like amber through the mist
is like a final strand
of golden hair that waves
within the current,

lashes out until it disappears.

She sails away from me,
lover to a desperate heart
with all my joys
and expectations anchored there,
like when a lover
turns to walk away
on a day of rain and grief,
robbing me of dreams.
I stare into the fog,
imagining that she's still there,
another beach or even just a light,
wanting desperately to catch
a final glimpse of where I was.

But sea meets sky uninterrupted,
their frontier edges blurred,
and once again I drift
upon unending waves.

SHIP OF SAND

Sailing on a ship of sand,
breaking through the waves
with the bow at 'Sconset
and standing on its tip,
I am captain
of this Nantucket ship,
my own destiny's maker:

explorer, fisherman, whaler.

But inevitably,
I'll face opposite the wind
and let it push me
towards civilization,
the realization
that I'm simply just a man
on a beach, after all.

METAMORPHOSIS

Today I watched a hapless swallowtail,
intermingled black and yellow movements
vivified with summer skill, set sail

until, with barbarous and ambushed sweep,
a tanager dove down and pulled it up
in frank aggression, and, as if to keep

the moment begging for its poignant end,
released its prey which panted up, spun round,
collapsed and struggled for its flight again.

Struck, carried for a bit, and then released,
a morbid dance performed before my eyes,
a vaulting dissonance of motion ceased

when reverberant designs, now blanched,
grew impotent and lost, imprisoned by
the crushing talons poised upon the branch,

kaleidoscopic wings pressed down and bruised,
perverse and twisted up behind itself,
a beauty ravishing and rent, subdued

by captor, muscular and virulent.
Down, up, thrust down again, the stout beak worked.
Wing-dust glittered like the faerie's remnant

innocence when startled into thin air,
as above, the tree leaves bounced and trembled
in the strain of violated nature.

Assaulted, butchered, leg by leg dismembered,
one by one plucked off to make digestion
smoother, a flying jewel sad-remembered

in the twilight of another day,
now gone, its two wings floated, lingered on,
beginning their descent into decay.

LITURGY

The roads are paved with dirt
instead of asphalt gold,
crushed and man-made rock.

The stones are untouched,
unformed into buildings,
those obtrusive dead things.

The tors stand brazen
with brio and buck,
yet unashamed to weep

their rivulet streams
or bleed the red clay
or revel in chartreuse,

and with a thousand trees
worship, casting them out,
a thousand liturgies.

MILKWEED FOR MONARCHS

I have seen the milkweed rise from roadsides
in July, rough as the back of hands
that know more work than rest.
Bitter runs the sap,
it oozes vile warning.
But still, the monarchs eat.
Soft mouths work rancorous,
ingesting pain to pay for flight.

Some mornings I'm the milkweed,
rooted where I did not choose,
weathered by the sun
and violating winds.
Some mornings I'm the larva,
taking in the rugged leaf,
trusting, without knowing,
that swallowing transforms.

We think joy must be sweet,
but monarchs know.
They eat what they receive.
They hang where they have found.
They grow where they are dark.

But when they rise into the August air,

there is no taste of leaf, just open sky,

and through a season's calm,

unspoken prayer,

they see the milkweed far below,

splitting rough-hewn husks,

and casting seeds

into the sunset's russet glow.

ABOUT THE AUTHOR

Seraphim George's work bridges nature, faith, and the human experience. He has published poetry in multiple literary journals and wrote an award-winning novel. Seraphim continues to write poetry and novels while working in Communications for non-profit organizations. He spends his free time in church, on the water, and in the written word, not to mention raising his three children with his wife, Juliana, and his cat, Kimchi. Milkweed for Monarchs is his first full-length poetry collection.

To read more of his work and find out more, you can visit www.seraphimgeorge.com.